Praise for Jon Curley's "New Shadows":

"The influential French thinker, Michel Foucault, elaborated on the concept of the "heterotopia" in an unpublished lecture he delivered in 1967, "Des Espace Autres/Of Other Spaces." For Foucault the heterotopia existed as a type of alternative space within society, as a site of resistance and otherness, holding out for the possibility of alternative thought. In this age of instant gratification and media-hype it is reassuring to encounter pockets of resistance, the concrete realisation of heterotopic space, in and through the productions of the small poetry press. It is surely a good thing to see publishers with such courage in their convictions to launch small, quality publications which provide a forum for new voices to be heard. One such press is Dos Madres, based in Ohio, who, in Jon Curley's *New Shadows*, provides us with a heterotopic space for which we should be grateful."

– Derek Coyle

"Curley's poetry calls on language's magic, its errancy, the thing that "sounds itself outside itself," as he writes, in his moving poem to Robert Duncan, one of his companionate shades or shadows. "Let the traces of our journey/be spliced into the under narrative," he continues. Almost everything in these beautiful and savvy poems plays at elusiveness, the old imprint in the sand replaced by a knotted, spectral presence equal and co-adjunct to an absence, "a ghost to its origin." Curley "sculpts shadows into substance," lovingly braiding emotion, humor and pain with independence and a sure authority."

– Michael Heller

"At an unfortunate pivotal point in history, the Bible's documentation of the Living Word simply ceased. It's everyone's mystery why those Books don't continue with tales of the year 5,770 when "Yuri begat Esther and persisted with God in their daily pilgrimage across the Williamsburg Bridge at dusk betwixt the invading hordes of social lepers and acrimonious philistines, and it was good" type stuff. Enter Jon Curley who heralds the prophets of Perpetuitous Chapters: Donleavy, Ringolevio, and all henceforth Passing Participants. And though each individual eurekic sharp yet flighty image he propounds can only spring forth from a poet whose feet connect directly to head, their assemblage together (which we assume must take place when said poet at some point sits) is often as thematically turbulent and viscerally cacaphonic as one would expect of the(se) ancient and ongoing Texts."

– Chris Leo

ANGLES
OF
INCIDENTS

by Jon Curley

DOS MADRES PRESS INC.

P.O.Box 294, Loveland, Ohio 45140

www.dosmadres.com   editor@dosmadres.com

Dos Madres is dedicated to the belief that the small press is essential to the vitality of contemporary literature as a carrier of the new voice, as well as the older, sometimes forgotten voices of the past. And in an ever more virtual world, to the creation of fine books pleasing to the eye and hand.

Dos Madres is named in honor of Vera Murphy and Libbie Hughes, the "Dos Madres" whose contributions have made this press possible.

Dos Madres Press, Inc. is an Ohio Not For Profit Corporation and a 501 (c) (3) qualified public charity. Contributions are tax deductible.

Executive Editor: Robert J. Murphy

Illustration & Book Design: Elizabeth H. Murphy
www.illusionstudios.net

Typset in Adobe Garamond Pro & Runy
ISBN 978-1-933675-83-1
Library of Congress Control Number: 2012944716

First Edition

ACKNOWLEDGEMENTS

"Death Valley," and "Hölderlin Revivivus: An Anniversary":
Talisman: Journal of Contemporary Poetry and Poetics.

Parts of "Stuttering Alphabetic Codex: Modern Multilingual
Historical Edition": *Otoliths*

"Metafizzles" and "Profiles": *Marshawk Review*

"Times in Rhymes, Ruins": *Meritage Press for the series
Hay(na)kus for Haiti*

Thank you to all these generous editors.

Special gratitude goes to Elena Alexander, Hedieh Allameh,
Jane Augustine, Zach Barocas, Kevin Bradbury, Derek Coyle,
David A. Fitschen, Michael Heller, Burt Kimmelman, Pam
LaMorra, David Morwick, Robert and Elizabeth Murphy, Pam
Rehm, the Beauchamps and the Curleys.

AUTHOR'S PHOTOGRAPH:
by
Hedieh Allameh

In Memory of Ann M. Curley and Samuel Menashe,
Mother and Poet, Guides through it All.

TABLE OF CONTENTS

Exhibit A

A penitent to perform

                    where reach is possible
      aglow within—

despite grace diffused, not
            demonstrated (erat…erratum)

            debilitated, the agonies
ranging across our lives, keen

to foster irreparable doubt conducive to harm

Flesh rides up the soul's stark prayer

Look anew at this predicament aslant,
           seen at an angle—

The Incidents in their accruals—

mark their shapes, collapse

    their frames—at least in mind

Emerge the momentary mercy (the prerogative
       is both structural and substantive)

Organize the prophetic stance
       Into healing prelude

while Now chimes in/with nightmare

The Evidence—

In dream, thought, obliterated,
    but still conscripted by baser world

These Incidents, incite-
    ments to revision

They are shadings of torrential consequence

They are Here...

Exhibit B

Here in the off-chance oblivion's staved off
    and ordinary life does not fixate itself too lovingly
    on itself we can herald some formulations
    encrypted as myth but trusted to us as forms
    through which to move

        Can we agree that deferring our obligations,
        those typical hesitations,
        only helps to beck us back to where we had come
    across (what did we come across?), return not
    to home but to the sites of suffering still waiting
    to be reoccupied?

    I am reluctant in our moments together to sing
    too loudly my lament, lament that is complaint
    which here shows restraint but really is exhaustion
    as these lines quench dis-ease with discourse
    thereby threatening their livelihoods

        Dead dividends, potentially

    Yet I do   and as the aperture through which I
    take stock dilates reckonings with the
    embossed narratives across dark territory
    I can glimpse a fragment, a few,

and note carefully that my exhibitions,

        these incidents are,

                                    were

the proofs of pain and possibility both

felt and remembered, even if

not visible

or not completely in view

yet. Until:

Why withdraw only to move back?
    The photograph of lack, specifically
the fadedness of you,
    all the sacred scratched surfaces,
age lines inadvertent, emulsified beyond
    recognition mostly

Recall that night under phosphorescent skies
    weighted, the stark suddenness of clouds
    dislocating into numerous trawled witnesses
    of your presence below, impressing
the friends there reveling with you just before
    the snap and flash: catastrophe

All we have is an outline of an outline, no
    forensics to distentangle your body
past and present, all figuration lurching between
    incandescence and oblivion, in-
significance and a signifier only in ruins
    for that is when your presence

Divided from us, divided between ghost
    and remembered presence
only an image or after-image
    your face now dimmer
blurred testimony that you occurred
    but elsewhere now and never again

Impacts

Like the house fire that consumed that poor family of four
    or the bicyclist hit at the intersection by a drunk
    or the immigrant worker drowned in concrete
    or the dog walker shocked dead by an electrified manhole cover
    or the homeless woman succumbing to pneumonia
    on a wintry night atop a city grate
    or all those woman slain in Ciudad Juarez
    or the victims of those hurricanes, meltdowns, and murders:

All those who fell down that hole where bodies
get lost, the language to claim them too,
decisive only in their loss, there is a shard of song
still preserved to lead them back to us if only
so we can story their absence with prayer
and glance back at where miracle and safekeeping
once kept us fixated to this world

Ejection Button, Life Term

The varieties of expulsions

    even tempered by prior arrangements

tend to exasperate. We wonder:

    How could we have been removed from this
pasture and its incidental light
cultivated, it seemed, only for nurturing

a quarantine from the septic boundaries

the terrestrial notion of sanctuary?

Solace has a gate and we went right through it

Now on the other side. Now this is where history
ignites like inverted prayer and we now endure
like ants rather than thrive like flowers
Until

    And yet

Monk Manner

For us who read
stark homilies
in pain, under
lacerating sun,
punishing moon,
lacing letters
of desperate yet
deliberate beatitudes
like Old Masters
despite seething attitudes
of world-at-war
& glimpse in heritage
some remaining qualities
to calm conditions
riddled with nerves & rot
we can only barely
summon the strength
which is enough
at least for Now
ministrations serving
in interest of miracle
are never to be mocked
even if mostly overlooked

Redemption Song

To save—

In the sense of spiritual economy; for sale, for
for salve, for save, saving, being,

To be savior, seeing succor, alm's makeover,
heart's takeover, to upend the isolato's ground
& furrow it with salt from the communal table

To be able, to be able to save, amid collapse,
under apse of oblivion or relapse, the tick-ticking
of symbolic bombs strafing sense, the deferred tense

Of waiting it out but not configuring it outward
into creation, creation of saving for saving creation,
there is no manual but no need, either,

To save—
        ways & means, beams, a way of building,
a form of kindling, only's kindliness,

                    —long live this

Body Politics

Stepping among the primary questions
the body is altered attention

Pam Rehm

Traumatic impulse in the brain, enhanced tremors
Of terrors, the night cries of the body contemplating
itself encased with mixed signals, chromosomal divination,
the faculty of predestination, preparing for cell division
to go libertarian, arbitrarily, subject to no fathomable
arbitration, the cancer secreting its cells, its selves
going haywire, re-wiring all to anarchy, where state
upends into mirage of sanity then goes weak with the
husbandry of self devouring self, genomic entropy
which calls for nothing but grief and utopia of the gone

fatalisms

Witness to the Furies
    I scramble for escape

They whittle down our world
   With a paring knife, disjointing our members
With the consideration of murderers

Use method to instigate death tropes
Calibrating systems of sensibility into seductive rhythms,

    Hymns, groundswells of accident, bad precedent,

Declensions and declaratives, those marauding narratives
which either deaden the spirit or the body or both

"Disaster" is their hiccup and their answer

Their provenance is not Greek tragic

Nor is it supernatural but theoretical,

Attributes of the non-heretical, foundational—
Stay away from them and their plans

Death Valley

Silence absorbs the reach. The whiteness
of these salt flats tends to emptiness.
Sky scans, seeps into the great distance.

Lie like the burdens of rock, christened
into a furious rusk, breeched
into crystallized counterparts,
glistening like mica,
be like the sense of this silence,
itself unsure of itself.

Now along the casual main grain
we find perhaps the striations
in the surface, forwarding a new face
whose sculpture is etched
into a view salt-licked
that embraces
that desolate ground space
as more likely than any
other feature or future that the rain-
soused mind could grow or imagine.

We reel in the expanse and find
masks discarded on the mountains.

Gods of rock found eternal time
to masquerade as the land they created
here. Homage to their work
is the etchings we leave as footprints,
as lived markers, as signatures
that express our silent appreciation
of craft resembling nature.

Stuttering Alphabetic Codex: Modern Multilingual Historical Edition

Gone and never to return
and being for myself alone
a remembrance of things to come
who fancied being a human.

Claude Roy

About
A boat
Ab oat
Ad out

Bunker
Bun cur
Bon coeur
Bann curb
Banned corps

Clandestine
Clandestiné
Clandesinée
Clan de sine

Depot
Deep po'
Depth soul
Death so
Death so

Efflorescence
E. fleur essence
Effervescence
Ever for vengeance

Futures
Few chores
Flew shores
Flue soars
Flu sores

Ghostly
Go hostly
Go hostilely
Go host spitably

Hindsight
Hind site
Hide sight
Hid night
Hit light

Internee
In turn we
In turn they
Internally

Jettison
Jetty sun
Jet sees some
Jester's son
Just her son

Kaleidoscope
Kollide o spark
Kollect all parts
Kollate all parts

Labelled
La belled
Labiled
Lay biled
Lab built

Monumental
My noumen tall
Mournumental
Mourn you meant well
More than we will

Navigate
Nave near gate
Never wait
Never waited

Orison
Or a son
Or a sun
Orus sung
Or war song

Prosopopoeia
Approprosopoeia
Apropos saw pouria
A pros so poor
A prose so sour

Quietude
Quiet tune
Quiet noon
Qui est une

Regulations
Reghoulations
Reekalations
Reckonings
Recognitions

Supervisor
Super visor
Soup is viler
Sweep this villager

Terror
T error
Terra or
Tear of war
Tear or war

Uniform
Uni form
Un if form
Uninformed

Vermiform
Vermin form
Verbal form
Verb I form
Verse ill formed

Watcher
Watch her
What was her
What was heard

16

Xhosa
Xerxes
Xerox
X-ray
X-raid

Yesterday
Yes to date
Yet err dei
Yer scene dies

Zoology
Zoo logos
Zone legend
Zeus legate
Zed abbatoir

Hölderlin Revivivus: An Anniversary

Divine shards of sense
                     or otherwise its equivalent:
a masquerade
       to flout logic's appeal to indictment, to definition,
the grief that grows in root
and routs—

       *   *   *

    "the exilic mind"
    —courier of "apocalyptica"—
which the poem envelopes in the mind
which the mind envelopes in the poem

"Near and
Hard to grasp, the god."

Hölderlin, I am now the age
which you saw fit—and saw you in fits—
for that ultimate abnegation
of common nutrients and normative lifestyle.

Was it a mad mood that made you immune—
or a Hamlet facemask to play the loon
so as to be free of tyrannies
of the wavering Tübingen sun
or that variable weather sonnet
exploding the little rooms in your head?

"I once asked the muse, and she
Replied:
You will find it in the end."

[Ah, this age (thirty six): this ache, this ague, this argument. I did not choose to rehearse or refuse conceivable medleys of personae in which to 1) inhabit; 2) discard; 3) utilize haphazardly, but my everyday encroaches with bewilderments– your plights become my plots. I see the symptoms of my worry and wariness, perhaps Time's jesting or the brain getting caught up in its fatigues, falling reveries, amnesias coming on too quickly.]

[On the subway I wonder where I am, where I am going. Every day the keys get lost, get found, go lost again, no longer turn the lock.]

For all I know, you condensed the fragile
fibers in your head into a shrouded sense field
better to ponder the interrelations of all
those historical and mythic marvels
you wished to unite, redeem, constitute
as a whole
        —a complex on which to balance
           the complex constituting yourself.

I am still with questions and
      I am still.

[My friends turnaway or else I no longer see(k)
them. One does not have to wait for dotage for
some sanctifying forces (of sanity) to go nil.]

      *   *   *

Performance as poetic need
Performance as plague
      (or vice versa)

Is this, was this, willful dissemblance
or the evaporation of your sanities?

Your face, as I caress it, seems strange.
Your mask, as I hold it, is flecked with fortitude.

      *   *   *

How to determine gesture from guise?
Stances both so spring-like and
like the dusk of fall.

Fall of mask?

I am still studying you, Friedrich,
for my own self is at risk,

[The transcription of my thoughts for the
past few weeks has been vexed, variable, and
I cannot concentrate on poems. On any-
thing. Self-diagnosis is a pitfall but all seems
symptomatic of disconnection, disaffection,
as if the mind is on fire. Questioning my
mental health over and over. What's wrong?
I keep it to myself. Much maddened grief.
Too many friends – or their loved ones – are
dying. Their lovers too.]

worrying itself into countenance
but still not knowing what it is.

You write:
            "Die Dichter müssen auch
            Die geistigen weltich seyn."
Translated:
            "Poets, too, men of spirit,
            Must keep to the world."

And I would add:

            "Spirits should not always obey gravities   [Manifestos no longer hit the
            and should fly up into the undestined tract   mark but heartfelt words may
            of their possible space."   release their aporias like shell-
                                                               tight casements of thought
                                                               instructed in mysteries and
—a space you now occupy   willing to rouse themselves
                        and maybe I.   like fists of light.]

Let's fly close to the surface   [I reach out for a young/old German
and strike out into the expanse—a new expanse.   poet; a summoning without closure
At the Danube's source, real or imagined, but   and not familiarly conclusive.]
redolent regardless, we shall find
the fructifying vigor of that river,   [And when I reach for the mask
that mask which we wash in the river,   it becomes yours. And we face (to
                                                               face) the facelessness: yet the eyes are
the mask that we take on and off interminably   there: piercing, not punishing, light
until the exhaustion hurts us,   gathering, almost pure]
and our own mad angels call us back.
                                                               [Better to wear a mask. Hope writes
                                                               a poem etched in an unrecognized
                                                               solvent.]

As I contemplate the piecemeal biographies & stenographies
which assert you as "this" or "that"—I ask what particulars
can be known. Is your mask inundated with sweat or the resin of a renegade?

                                                               [I've a devil's chance of knowing who
                                                               I was when I set out to be he who
                                                               was instigatior, excavator, of you.
                                                               Not the need for communication
                                                               but for the sustenance of strangers.
                                                               Yes, that is what I am seeking.]

20

Blake in 1989

The walls fell. Most ceilings
trembled. Foundations floundered.
Some sundered, some stayed the same.

The firmament was still an umbrella.
Under it, rained change. The watchtower
became voyeur, yet its beacon still
burned. Flies crowded to its beam.

That nine-year old girl in the crowd,
near the ramparts, imagines herself
a goddess, wandering through
dead furnishings, new futurities.
She wonders how the walls that fell
could keep propped their fearful lies.

I whisper phantoms in her ears.

Failed Faculties

Aspirin or Hemlock?—What is the remedy
for the "abscess of thought" or the contagion
located in our nodal night?

Diseases are communicable. Consequently,
we communicate only diseased messages.

Our current placards are plaque-ridden
and the broadscasts epistemologically cast
us in uncharted immunological places.

I'm infected. I've lost my choice. A pox
on the language: the voice's virus
eats away at the tongue which created
the mind. I try to speak.

No longer can I create networks to chisel
gullets through which to pour words.
The voice and its wires are gnarled.
What can be written—as here recorded—
is a voice unvoiced, its thought diseased.
Disused. The remedies cannot be those voiced
or written. I remain unmended, unmade.

Silence breeds its progeny, the mutation
of which might proliferate cells to bridge
brain, mouth, and word. Healing would
be a holiness, fusing sound and sense
in triage, in language, in the fragile
translation of sickness into health.

For now, I await the cure and the
analysis, the environ/mental catalysts
for this condition, a gesture of
the gesture-less, out of the disquieted quiet.

Surface Burns

Codes of contact go splat, rejoinders to our misinterpretations,
non-worships, our workshops in which we forge farrago
rather than soft powders of imago to trace the I's we might have been

beneath the skin, deep in core's cortex, just above the hybrid heart
which circulates sentiments and sediments alike, red on red,
lies the hypersensitive disguise machine, no deceiver,

not at all, but the believer that no dimmer switch attaches
to the imaginary capillaries that are not imaginary at all
and concoct through us, x-ray like, a domain of subterranean,

subcutaneous engineers plying the huge crates of wonder,
separate but equal to biology, the angel's share of invention,
immaterial, the real within the real, always reeling.

Grand Man

Hard to believe this many years dead—
I shadowed him tenderly, teasing
his freckled fists from the newspaper,
summoning attention from the farmer boy
turned baker, to make stories about
fields and cakes, take me on long ago
frolics to other lands, holding me in hand
as he walked with a hawthorn cane from
the rocking chair to another distant plane.

Clan Initiation

Skeptics will draw blood from facts
and spray you in the face with contours
corrugated by demands, exacting demands.
Remedy these crass designs by setting fire
to your own brand of non-facts, letting
their smoke herald the dawning of the Tribe
in the direction of the light—inner, outer,
& out of sight.

Metafizzles

corona
seeks immensity
of peace's pleroma

gnostic
nostrums of
illuminated manuscripts ripped

heretics
have heritage
in heart's healing

codex
composed discomposed
written rewritten revised

two
martyrs turned
on burning wheels

if
one should
stay soul, shade

imprimatur
your flesh
penned rosy filigrees

whether
fathom beyond
still defy gravity

cannot
see so
mind wears visions

next
place new
grace for All

Weil
wore woe
weal like wheel

lustrations
pour rain
onto mire (mine)

afresh
flowers bloom
from thorn crowns

meaning
no matter
in the hereafter

sightings
of no
saints just selves

rainbow-
beaked revenants
inscribed beside text

from
cloister to
coracle, sail on

summons
where you
seek new thoughts

fructify
benevolence growing
misshapen in present

end
no end
bend in path

Profiles

how
Howe's words
whir into souls

when
Samuel Menashe
lost for afternoon

Heaney
hastened poetic
practice in me

Medbh
at NYU
a randy lass

Nuala
saved me
from my selves

Kimmelman's
mother poem
on Garrison Keillor!

Welshman
R.S. Thomas
at final reading

Heller
my mentor
means much more

Augustine
not saint
but poet Jane

Otoliths
inner ear
definitely Mark Young

Silliman
no silly
man, a thunderstorm

Talisman
Ed fosters
no frivolous work

speaking
tongues with
her hands: Lauterbach

scribe
describes Finkelstein's
sacred text, vocation

saw
Tabios at
Poets House: wow!

jazzman
Paul Pines
actually sonic poet

Austin's
Gg Re
a mischief monument

missed
the "the"—
Les Murray's poem!

Gizzi
almost taught
me, the Unteachable

Thom
Gunn never
responded: no postage?

Times in Rhymes, Ruins

disaster
cannot be
written but mimicked

natural
disasters? no
causes so conventional

L'Ouverture,
there's great
need of you

Miltonic
global crisis
renders Haiti Hades

global
capitalism like
Goya's devouring father

elliptical
the whims
of states, malevolent

tabloids
interest world
suffering a palimpsest

Greene's
The Comedians:
laughter long gone

gravediggers
find a
beating heart, shine

entrenchments
enchantments ghost
Haiti's hurt history

disregard
of citizens
afar a sacrilege

sacred
the share
we tether together

ecologies
of fear
override our borders

temptation
to darkness
tempered by hope

politics:
a viper
in a vase

N.G.O's
often puppets
of mediocre masters

to
restore world
return harmonic convergences

my
socialist heart
and anarchist mind

saving
grace? dispense
it, distribute it

my
sisters brothers
Haitian half-moons majestic

Archaelogy of Facsimile

Perplexed and depressed, occasionally startled,
    half-stuck in episodic shock
watching unreeling the septic news of Syria,
    massacres repeated with the fastidiousness
of the casual, careful occurrence,
    I entertain the lore of Enki
who advised the manufacture of humans
    from clay and blood, unaware
of designs encoded pre-birth
    to dry clay and spray blood,
sunder the experiment, make mischief
    of the human by the human,
make all mythology moot by this redundancy
    and us to learn our roots
back to clay, back in blood.

Polarities

Intersecting angles
the imposture of doubt
bordering the premise
colliding with self-impression

I stagger over and over
at the rupture line of tension and release
words and movement
wishing for errancy and ardency

a way out, flies and specks
stirring, capturing the technique
with no vision when vision is required

the tabula rasa needing raising, light wiping,
and to be turned over and over again.

Existents and Precipitants

Like watching the scene from an angle
As it stretches itself out, grows anamorphic
And between the bodies and their outlines
You can see the widening inner spaces growing
Outer, indications of ingenious layering effects
of perception which, if stripped, reveal the sub-
phenomena of aura, arriving into this world
from some others:

These we can call the angels of incidence

Snap Shots

Caught in the cross-hairs,
integuments blur

The rush for resolution
or focused apprehension
(what observers call attention)
stymied by the atmospheric pulse
that threatens to expand or contract
objects as dimensions derange

This too is how people go missing:
not instant disappearance,
but gradually, slipping
away or through
cracks of images
enforced rather than extracted

Dislocation of the visible provokes
the ghosts in flesh to gather, to tear
asunder the fact of matter

No Quarter

So as not to offend sunbathers
those drowned gypsy children
were covered in beach towels,
left to rot there on the coastline,
thin limbs exposed and articulated
like wood beams hammered
at right angles, the geometry
of neglect, residing just next to
suntan oil, suburban excess, Sunday
newspapers. The laws of some cruelties
hardly alter. And the dispossessed
move along, not away, from such
indifferent precincts, haunting
the earth without upsetting it,
covered and uncovered, here and there.

Pax

Never mention God unless God
gives permission. But God never
gives permission. Silence is a god.

From this angle—

myth merging with matter
genesis of new noumen
the spark of science against story
narrative spliced for two trails

From this angle—

solid objects less so
eros weighted, waiting to grow
"profane existence," the revel of renewal
the contours of heart redefined as fact

From this angle—

elective affinities charged haphazardly
permitting grace, guaranteeing charge
practical applications, not theoretical asides

From this angle—

temptation to see stasis
as objective correlative
denied credibility as
momentum quickens the pulse,
shatters the ice

From this angle—

masks half-melted help
persona gravitate past
artifice into otherwise,
"other wise": another way
for face to reveal face

From this angle—

objects in the mirror
appear closer than they are
because negative theology,
wish fulfillment

From this angle—

the mechanisms of statecraft
still inspire disdain,
ploughshares still
a version of counter-plan

From this angle—

all contents have shifted
all figurations have reframed
the mirror seems to be gaining images

From this angle—

the topography of toil
is peopled still by suffering
the prayerful pleas remain in place

From this angle—

convergence of coincidence
recommends a steady diet
of accident, upending
the linear for
the uncurling curve

From this angle—

the illuminated manuscript shines
unstintingly then burns itself
up so its atoms can be eaten
food of the gods

From this angle—

the birds are sharpening their beaks
to break open the seeds
to plant new, needed visions

From this angle—

the agony of autonomy can
be alleviated by droplets
of community, sub-
lingually administered,
three times a day

From this angle—

you carry the light
with the endurance of a goddess
so too your beauty

From this angle—

the shudder of illogic
carries its scream
across continents,
piercing the ear
drums of most animals

From this angle—

cardiac arrhythmia occurs
when poems are prohibited
by their makers to follow
their own lines, all the time

From this angle—

Arab Spring might enjoy
the renaissance of flowers
in the summer of expectation

From this angle—

orisons on the horizon
merely clouds
encased in holy air

From this angle—

we may break the confines
of this place and that
with less attention to real estate
and more to the estate
of the real

From this angle—

the tears shed in the tears shed
become cooling waters into which
fish of the future find station

From this angle—

the aggravated assault of the spectacle
becomes a cover for more careful thought
that dreams the unimagined
into a vehicle for voice

From this angle—

evers and elsewheres yield
greater returns than eventuals
and conditionals,
remaining steadfast in their faith

From this angle—

containment and not alignment
seems a torrential sin
what other ways to find means
that give shelters, not quarantines?

From this angle—

the despair that seems motivated
by hunger is in fact the decision
to keep the saline wash
as cleansing agent in flow
despite where other thoughts
might grow

From this angle—

I cannot see you but I can trust you
as the analogics we encountered
in those years in the desert
delivered us from it and from
ourselves and birthed eyes
on the back of our intuitions
and gave us a nod to the night
but not evil

From this angle—

a butterfly with arched wings
glowing with words showing
us worlds to know, not
knowing that the crucial
codex is flying with it
and in us too

From this angle—

the angle opens itself up
to various angles, many
possibilities, more often
then not and not ever
relenting in doing so

From this angle—

the angles of incidents
are the angels of incidence
and they address each
other like lines ever-
lasting, interwining,
measuring the degrees
to which we are
flying between
histories and imaginaries,
gaining ground and air,
and all between

ABOUT THE AUTHOR

Jon Curley's first volume of poems, *New Shadows*, was published in 2009 by Dos Madres Press. He is a senior university lecturer of Humanities at the New Jersey Institute of Technology and has published a book of criticism, *Poets and Partitions: Confronting Communal Identities in Northern Ireland* (Sussex Academic Press, 2011). In addition to teaching, Curley works with children at Battery Park in New York City, just across from Poets House, and leads walking tours about nature and poetry.

BOOKS BY DOS MADRES PRESS

Jennifer Arin - *Ways We Hold* (2012)

Michael Autrey - *From The Genre Of Silence* (2008)

Paul Bray - *Things Past and Things to Come* (2006), *Terrible Woods* (2008)

Jon Curley - *New Shadows* (2009)

Richard Darabaner - *Plaint* (2012)

Deborah Diemont - *Wanderer* (2009), *Diverting Angels* (2012)

Joseph Donahue - *The Copper Scroll* (2007)

Annie Finch - *Home Birth* (2004)

Norman Finkelstein - *An Assembly* (2004), *Scribe* (2009)

Gerry Grubbs - *Still Life* (2005), *Girls in Bright Dresses Dancing* (2010)

Richard Hague - *Burst, Poems Quickly* (2004)

Pauletta Hansel - *First Person* (2007), *What I Did There* (2011)

Michael Heller - *A Look at the Door with the Hinges Off* (2006),
    Earth and Cave (2006)

Michael Henson - *The Tao of Longing & The Body Geographic* (2010)

R. Nemo Hill - *When Men Bow Down* (2012)

W. Nick Hill - *And We'd Understand Crows Laughing* (2012)

Eric Hoffman - *Life At Braintree* (2008), *The American Eye* (2011)

James Hogan - *Rue St. Jacques* (2005)

Keith Holyoak - *My Minotaur* (2010), *Foreigner* (2012)

David M. Katz - *Claims of Home* (2011)

Burt Kimmelman - *There Are Words* (2007), *The Way We Live* (2011)

Richard Luftig - *Off The Map* (2006)

Austin MacRae - *The Organ Builder* (2012)

J. Morris - *The Musician, Approaching Sleep* (2006)

Rick Mullin - *Soutine* (2012)

Robert Murphy - *Not For You Alone* (2004), *Life in the Ordovician* (2007)

Pam O'Brien - *The Answer To Each Is The Same* (2012)

Peter O'Leary - *A Mystical Theology of the Limbic Fissure* (2005)

Bea Opengart - *In The Land* (2011)

David A. Petreman - *Candlelight in Quintero - bilingual edition* (2011)

Paul Pines - *Reflections in a Smoking Mirror* (2011)

David Schloss - *Behind the Eyes* (2005)

William Schickel - *What A Woman* (2007)

Lianne Spidel & Anne Loveland - *Pairings* (2012)
Murray Shugars - *Songs My Mother Never Taught Me* (2011)
Nathan Swartzendruber - *Opaque Projectionist* (2009)
Jean Syed - *Sonnets* (2009)
Madeline Tiger - *The Atheist's Prayer* (2010), *From the Viewing Stand* (2011)
James Tolan - *Red Walls* (2011)
Henry Weinfield - *The Tears of the Muses* (2005),
     Without Mythologies (2008), *A Wandering Aramaean* (2012)
Donald Wellman - *A North Atlantic Wall* (2010)
Martin Willetts Jr. - *Secrets No One Must Talk About* (2011)
Tyrone Williams - *Futures, Elections* (2004), *Adventures of Pi* (2011)

www.dosmadres.com